WORLDS MOST PRACTICAL BOOK FOR SALES PERSONS

THE INCREDIBLE CLOER

3 HACKS FOR ULTIMATE SALES SUCCE$S

The First and only Book that Reveals Your Proven Method

KP CHATURVEDI

BlueRose ONE.com
Stories Matter
NewDelhi • London

BLUEROSE PUBLISHERS
India | U.K.

BlueRose ONE
Stories Matter
NewDelhi • London

For permissions requests or inquiries regarding this publication, please contact:

BLUEROSE PUBLISHERS
www.BlueRoseONE.com
info@bluerosepublishers.com
+91 8882 898 898
+4407342408967

ISBN: 978-93-5704-780-7

Cover design: Muskan Sachdeva
Typesetting: Rohit

First Edition: January 2025

DEDICATION

This book is dedicated to my Parents & all my teachers & mentors for believing in me and encouraging me to move ahead in life to follow my dreams.

"I would like to extend my heartfelt gratitude to my esteemed mentor, Mr. Rajat Katyal. His invaluable guidance and support have been instrumental in shaping my sales strategy and approach. Under his mentorship, I have gained the skills and confidence to excel in sales and create value for others. Thank you to him for believing in me and helping me unlock my potential."

About Sales....

Sales is one of the best nobel professions of the world. Sales is not only a number game or manipulation skill or persuasive job.

I landed in this profession without any prior planning and I am pretty sure about the sales representatives or sales officers or territory sales incharge of any industry (whether it is pharma, fmcg, consumer durable, building material, insurance, banking, home improvement or any others) including you, are in this profession. they never dreamed of making a career in sales nor their parents thinked of.

From the time you get up in the morning until the time you go to bed at night, you are continually doing part of the sales job, negotiating, communicating, persuading, influencing and trying to get people to cooperate with you to do the things that you want them to do.

If you are poor at sales, then you are merely a recipient of influence. This means that you will be continually influenced and persuaded by others. If you are good at sales, it means that you will be an agent of influence and you will be constantly influencing and persuading others in the direction that you want them to go.

All effective parents are wonderful salespeople. All effective children are very good at selling ideas to their parents. Excellent employees are very effective at getting their bosses to do things, and getting their coworkers to go along with them and cooperate with them in getting the job done. Everyone who is effective in virtually any area of life that involves other people is an excellent salesperson of some kind

Even selling has a bad rap in our society but always remember (if you hate sales you hate success) no parents want their kids to grow up to be a sales-person . During my college time many of my colleagues were saying sales is something they never want to do in their careers and **yet they say sales is the most fundamental skill.**

Yes it is right, as I said earlier in the top, sales is world's best profession and skill, it's not only manipulation its a

- ✔ Serving
- ✔ Educating
- ✔ Guiding
- ✔ Helping
- ✔ Consulting
- ✔ Analyzing
- ✔ Supporting

No matter in which profession you are doing a part of sales in your day-to-day job.

I highly recommend to all graduates and working professionals to be aware about this high demanding skill.

Here you will get the beauty of adopting the changes, as you know change is the only universal truth which is constantly happening time after time.

you will get the opportunity to know & learn the different cultures and geographies which will open the door to your personal as well professional growth.

It is something where you will get the chance to serve or add value to someone's life. It will open the door to increase the network personally as well as professionally.

And you might know your network is your net worth.

So enjoy the profession & Be UNSTOPPABLE..

And one more important area of life if you did not find passion of your life

Till date, then I highly recommend you make it your PASSION after the 10 years I guarantee you will say thank you to me.

Contents

SECTION - 1

THE 3 PILLARS

You know majority of sales persons are thinking like that:

I am not good at selling, I never thought to work in the Sales profession, I am not satisfied with the revenue I am generating from my incentives/ commissions/perks through generating Sales.

As a Sales champion/ coach to colleagues and 100+ new learners over the past few years, I have heard this often from Sellers/ Entrepreneurs during my one-on-one interactions.

Every Single Sales Representative / Entrepreneurs, and that includes you, has the potential to accelerate your Sales Career or Business through the new GAME™ plan and become a Millionaire Seller.

However, what separates those who become Millionaire Sellers and those who don't are the Right Skills they chose to master.

Through my hardcore work experience of 15+ years with the B2b & B2C and learnt from some of my mentors, I have found out 3 Pillars every Millionaire Seller needs to master.

And, with this book, my wholehearted promise to you is to help you discover those hacks that are the 3 Pillars.

THE MAGIC OF THE 3 PILLARS- MAP

MINDSET

APPROACH

PROCESS

The reason I call these 3 Pillars and not 3 Steps/ Skills is pretty simple.

All the three areas are strong characteristics that are used for supporting Sales and building up to the next level.

Many Sales Executives/ Entrepreneurs struggle with their Sales because they are running after the greatest **manipulative Strategy in their industry.**

Sales is a job, which is full of rejection day after day & month after month.

This can hurt your self-respect or self-esteem and it can seed a self -doubt over your capabilities. However, if you have already decided to overcome all the resistance and decided to be successful, it means you understand the power of mindset for successful selling.

You are known about how to shift into a growth mentality and you are well known about using the opportunities of rejection which means those learnings from rejection and those practical learnings will lead you to create a great successful story in sales.

So Here Comes the first pillar that is **Your Mindset**.

If you ask 100 sales people to define the term "selling ," you will probably get 100 different answers, and in this case, that's ninety-five too many. The correct definition of selling is probably implementing the best approach to your sales process as a definition. Why is this so important? Because your beliefs drive your behavior, and beliefs evolve from mindset, and if you do not have the right mindset with the right definition of selling, you will not have the skills and tools needed to succeed. You can bring a baseball bat to a football game, but you or your team will not score touchdowns with it and will probably get thrown out.

Mindset refers to a person's attitude, beliefs, and way of thinking. It can be categorized into three types:

Fixed Mindset

Growth Mindset

Service Mindset

A fixed mindset is when someone believes that their abilities, intelligence, and talents are fixed traits that cannot be changed. They tend to avoid challenges and give up easily when faced with obstacles. They also tend to compare themselves with others and seek validation from external sources.

On the other hand, a growth mindset is when someone believes that their abilities, intelligence, and talents can be developed through hard work, dedication, and perseverance. They embrace challenges and view failures as opportunities to learn and grow.

They also focus on their own progress and development, rather than comparing themselves with others.

Having a growth mindset can lead to greater success and fulfillment in life. It allows individuals to set goals, take risks, and learn from their mistakes. It also promotes a sense of resilience and determination when faced with challenges.

Developing a growth mindset requires self-awareness, effort, and practice. It involves recognizing and challenging limiting beliefs, setting achievable goals, and embracing the learning process. By adopting a growth mindset, individuals can unlock their full potential and achieve their goals.

Service Mindset

A service mindset refers to an attitude or approach that prioritizes delivering excellent customer service. It involves understanding and meeting the needs and expectations of customers, and going above and beyond to ensure their satisfaction.

Having a service mindset is important for businesses and organizations that rely on customer satisfaction to succeed. It involves treating every customer with respect, empathy, and kindness, and striving to exceed their expectations.

Some key characteristics of a service mindset include:

1. **Empathy**: Understanding and relating to the needs and feelings of customers.
2. **Active listening**: Paying close attention to customers' concerns and feedback, and responding appropriately.
3. **Problem-solving**: Being proactive in identifying and solving customer problems and concerns.

4. **Continuous improvement**: Seeking feedback and continuously improving processes and services to better meet customer needs.
5. **Positive attitude**: Maintaining a positive and solution-focused attitude, even in challenging situations.

Developing a service mindset requires training, coaching, and a commitment to customer satisfaction. It involves creating a culture of service excellence within an organization, where everyone from frontline employees to senior leaders is focused on delivering exceptional customer service.

By adopting a service mindset, businesses and organizations can build strong relationships with customers, increase loyalty and retention, and ultimately drive growth and success.

So the next set of pillars is about Your **Approach.**

The sale is not manipulated work. But it is a combination of building a logical connection and then an emotional connection, and that is what some frustrated colleagues in the profession fail to grasp. Sales is like a competitive game and challenging too.

So it is very necessary to adopt the right approach and that is also a reflection of your habits . So you can see the habits play an important role to have a successful approach, both are interconnected. You can not approach any one randomly for your sales or we can say you can not display the successful characteristics in your behavior randomly.. So that means, without the right habits , you can not plan the right approach for your sales process.

The way you connect with people has changed. The old approach does not work anymore . You know the old time and the old way has changed as well. Trust has always had to be earned, but today's consumer has become more cautious and skeptical than ever before.

Yes, it's exhausting and sometimes annoying, especially when you live in a society of experts backed by nothing but Google, but the fact remains that consumers do not want to be chatted up and sold to, they want to be talked to, asked, listened to and above all understood. Dale Carnegie said that 85% of our decisions are emotional and 15% are logical. Unless you are on a game show, people do not like interrogation and answering a plethora of questions.

As sales is one of the challenging professions, you need to update yourself accordingly.

People don't know what they want until you show it to them.

\- **Steve Jobs**

This way of approaching requires the salesperson to focus on selling the solution, not the product.

You can't assure the customer wants what you have to offer and just walk in there and expect an order.

If I talk about the old method of approaching for sales, It was AIDA, where

A stood for "Attention." The first part of the old model was getting the attention of the prospect;

I stood for "Interest." The salesperson aroused interest by discussing features of the product;

D stood for "Desire." Desire was aroused by discussing the benefits of the product:

A stood for "Action." After arousing interest and desire, the salesperson asked for an action commitment by the customer.

But in this sales revolution especially after the pandemic this old model is not working because you have to understand that you are selling value, not price and Questions persuade more powerfully than any other form of verbal behavior.

Also There is a clear statistical association between the use of questions and the success of the interaction.

In the current model of Selling, the discovery phase (Need or Desire identification) is a key step.

So I have created the ultimate model of selling after spending 15 + years in the sales profession, working with both the channels

B2B & B2C. So I want to show the comparison graph of old and this ultimate sales model QCVC.

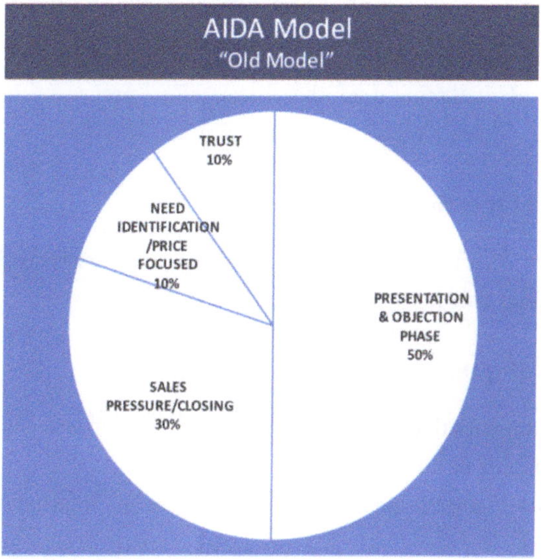

Vs.

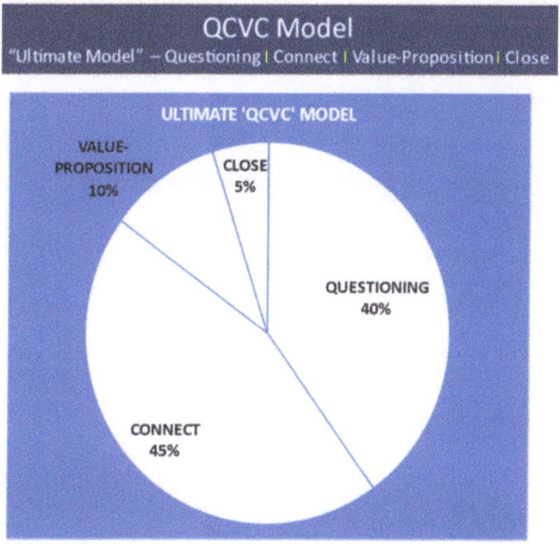

Here the question is all about the discovery phase. We do need identification/ discovery by questioning and this is not only open ended or closed ended questions. It's all about persuasive questioning.

Here's an explanation of the 4-step sales process: Questions, Connect, Value Proposition, and Closing:

Step 1: Questions (Discovery)

Purpose: Gather information about the customer's needs, pain points, and goals.

Types of questions:

1. Open-ended questions: Encourage the customer to share their thoughts and feelings.
2. Closed-ended questions: Gather specific information and clarify details.
3. Probing questions: Dive deeper into the customer's needs and pain points.

Best practices:

1. Listen actively and attentively to the customer's responses.
2. Take notes to reference later in the conversation.
3. Avoid asking leading questions or making assumptions.

Step 2: Connect (Building Rapport)

Purpose: Establish a relationship with the customer, build trust, and create a positive atmosphere.

Ways to connect:

1. Find common ground: Share a personal experience or interest.

2. Show genuine interest: Ask about the customer's business goals, or challenges.
3. Use positive body language: Maintain eye contact, smile, and use open and approachable nonverbal cues.

Best practices:

1. Be authentic and genuine in your approach.
2. Avoid coming across as insincere or manipulative.
3. Keep the conversation balanced and focused on the customer.

Step 3: Value Proposition (Presenting the Solution)

Purpose: Clearly and concisely communicate the value of your product or service and how it addresses the customer's needs.

Key elements:

1. Clearly define the problem or pain point.
2. Explain how your solution addresses the problem.
3. Highlight the benefits, features, and unique value proposition.

Best practices:

1. Tailor your value proposition to the customer's specific needs and pain points.
2. Use storytelling and examples to illustrate the value of your solution.
3. Avoid using jargon or technical terms that might confuse the customer.

Step 4: Closing (Securing the Sale)

Purpose: Confidently and professionally ask for the sale, address any objections, and finalize the agreement.

Closing techniques:

The Alternative of Choice: Present your solution as the best option.

1. The Summary Close: Recap the key points and benefits.
2. The Assumptive Close: Assume the sale and discuss implementation details.
3. Best practices:
4. Be confident and assertive when asking for the sale.
5. Anticipate and address objections in a clear and concise manner.
6. Ensure all parties are clear on the terms and conditions of the sale.

By mastering these 4 steps, salespeople can effectively navigate the sales process, build strong relationships with customers, and drive successful outcomes.

The Discovery part of the sales process is crucial in understanding the customer's needs, pain points, and goals. Here's a more detailed explanation of the Discovery step:

Types of Discovery Questions

1. Open-Ended Questions: Encourage the customer to share their thoughts and feelings.

   Example: "Can you tell me more about your current challenges?"

2. Closed-Ended Questions: Gather specific information and clarify details.

   Example: "What is your current budget for this project?"

3. Probing Questions: Dive deeper into the customer's needs and pain points.

   Example: "Can you elaborate on what you mean by 'inefficient processes'?"

4. Clarifying Questions: Ensure understanding and avoid assumptions.

   Example: "Just to confirm, you're looking for a solution that can integrate with your existing system?"

Best Practices for Discovery

1. Listen Actively: Pay attention to the customer's responses and take notes.
2. Avoid Assumptions: Don't assume you know the customer's needs or pain points.
3. Stay Neutral: Avoid taking a biased or leading approach during the discovery process.
4. Use a Structured Approach: Use a framework or template to guide the discovery conversation.

Benefits of Effective Discovery

1. Improved Understanding: Gain a deeper understanding of the customer's needs and pain points.
2. Increased Trust: Build trust with the customer by demonstrating a genuine interest in their challenges.
3. Better Solution Alignment: Ensure that the proposed solution aligns with the customer's needs and goals.
4. Reduced Objections: Anticipate and address potential objections during the discovery process.

The Connect step of the sales process is crucial in building a relationship with the customer and establishing a foundation for trust and credibility. Here's a more detailed explanation of the Connect step:

Why Connect is Important

1. Builds Trust: Establishing a personal connection helps build trust with the customer.
2. Creates Rapport: Finding common ground or shared interests creates a positive atmosphere.
3. Differentiates You: Connecting with the customer on a personal level differentiates you from competitors.

Ways to Connect with Customers

1. Find Common Ground: Look for shared interests, hobbies, or experiences.
2. Show Genuine Interest: Ask questions and listen actively to the customer's responses.
3. Use Positive Body Language: Maintain eye contact, smile, and use open and approachable nonverbal cues.
4. Use Storytelling: Share personal anecdotes or stories that illustrate your expertise and build rapport.

Best Practices for Connecting

1. Be Authentic: Be genuine and true to yourself in your interactions.
2. Listen Actively: Pay attention to the customer's responses and show that you're engaged.
3. Avoid Being Too Pushy: Don't come across as overly aggressive or pushy.
4. Follow Up: After the initial meeting, follow up with the customer to continue building the relationship.

Benefits of Connecting

1. Increased Trust: Building a personal connection increases trust and credibility.
2. Improved Communication: Connecting with the customer improves communication and ensures that both parties are on the same page.
3. Increased Loyalty: Customers who feel connected to a salesperson are more likely to remain loyal.
4. Better Sales Outcomes: Connecting with the customer increases the likelihood of a successful sale.

The Value Proposition is a critical step in the sales process, as it clearly communicates the value of your product or service to the customer. Here's a more detailed explanation of the Value Proposition:

What is a Value Proposition?

A Value Proposition is a clear and concise statement that explains how your product or service addresses the customer's needs, pain points, and goals. It highlights the unique benefits, features, and value that your solution provides.

Key Elements of a Value Proposition

1. Problem Statement: Clearly define the problem or pain point that the customer is facing.
2. Solution Overview: Provide a brief overview of your product or service and how it addresses the customer's problem.
3. Key Benefits: Highlight the unique benefits and value that your solution provides, such as cost savings, increased efficiency, or improved outcomes.
4. Unique Selling Points (USPs): Emphasize what sets your product or service apart from competitors.

5. Proof Points: Provide evidence, such as case studies, testimonials, or data, to support the value proposition.

Best Practices for Communicating a Value Proposition

1. Keep it Simple and Concise: Avoid using jargon or technical terms that might confuse the customer.
2. Focus on Benefits, Not Features: Emphasize how your solution will benefit the customer, rather than just listing its features.
3. Use Storytelling Techniques: Use anecdotes, examples, or metaphors to make the value proposition more relatable and memorable.
4. Tailor the Value Proposition: Customize the value proposition to the customer's specific needs, pain points, and goals.

Benefits of a Strong Value Proposition

1. Differentiation: A clear and compelling value proposition differentiates your product or service from competitors.
2. Increased Customer Engagement: A well-crafted value proposition resonates with customers and increases their engagement and interest.
3. Improved Sales Outcomes: A strong value proposition increases the likelihood of a successful sale by clearly communicating the value and benefits of your solution.

Close the Sale Securing the sale is the final step in the sales process, where you ask for the customer's commitment to purchase your product or service. Here are some key strategies and best practices to help you secure the sale:

Strategies for Securing the Sale

1. The Alternative of Choice: Present your solution as the best option for the customer.
2. The Summary Close: Recap the key points and benefits of your solution.
3. The Assumptive Close: Assume the sale and discuss implementation details.
4. The Trial Close: Ask for a small commitment or trial to test the solution.
5. The Upsell/Cross-Sell: Offer additional products or services that complement the initial sale.

Best Practices for Securing the Sale

1. Be Confident: Show confidence in your solution and its value.
2. Use Positive Language: Use positive and enthusiastic language when asking for the sale.
3. Anticipate Objections: Anticipate and address potential objections before asking for the sale.
4. Use Scarcity: Create a sense of urgency by highlighting limited-time offers or scarcity.
5. Provide a Clear Call-to-Action: Clearly state what you're asking the customer to do next.

Common Objections and How to Overcome Them

1. Price: Highlight the value and benefits of your solution, and offer flexible pricing options.
2. Features: Emphasize the key features and benefits that meet the customer's needs.
3. Timing: Highlight the importance of acting quickly to achieve the desired outcomes.
4. Uncertainty: Provide case studies, testimonials, or data to alleviate concerns and build trust.

Finalizing the Sale

1. Confirm the Details: Review and confirm the sale details, including pricing, delivery, and implementation.
2. Provide a Clear Next Steps: Outline the next steps and timeline for implementation.
3. Thank the Customer: Express gratitude for the customer's business and trust.
4. Follow Up: Schedule a follow-up meeting or call to ensure a smooth implementation and to address any concerns.

If you want to be a great closer and then you have to build trust, credibility with the other person.

Empathy is one of the top factors for building connections with the buyer and if you are the master in empathizing easily & faster then no one could stop you from closing the sale.

After this I would like to show you, the top 4 tactics for boosting the value of your approach considering the selling time:

1. Prequalify prospects before you engage with them.
2. No random approach on a prospect unexpectedly.
3. Reduce focus with time-consuming clients.
4. Convert customer relationships into long term association.

Now as we all know we are living in the revolutionary age specially after covid pandemic.

Everything is changed, you need to be a result oriented sales professional, so here comes your **PROCESS** ,this is the third Pillar.

PROCESS

The biggest problem in sales is the problem you do not know you have. Excuse me? Read that again, because it is remarkably meaningful and true. It also speaks of the absolute necessity of self-knowledge, cluelessness and a subway token will not get you very far. The key to growth and development is self-knowledge. If you do not know what your biggest problem is, you are in a real bind, and in sales, that bind is the equivalent of a hung-up call or a slammed door in your face. If you do not know what the problem is, how can you solve it? You can not, but once you identify the problem, you can and will change your situation. Think about your best teachers. They were inspiring, motivating and made you think, right? Great salespeople are like your favorite teachers. They inform, involve, engage and make you think . They interact. They make connections, and as high-tech as things are these days, selling is like school, preferably person-to-person, not virtual.

(but sometimes this is the only viable option). It is critical that any salesperson keep up with the way people want to be sold. It's not about having the right product. It's about having the right method and the right solution or process. "People hate to be sold, but they love to buy" It's called the sales process for a reason. We all want our product and services to go viral, but that will not happen if we have the wrong process. We have all been at this point and want to help you avoid it at all costs. If this is where you currently are,

Mix the elements to gain new solution-oriented insights until you wake up with the epiphany that changes your perception and that leads to solution-oriented **process,**

Below diagram will help you more about Sales Process...

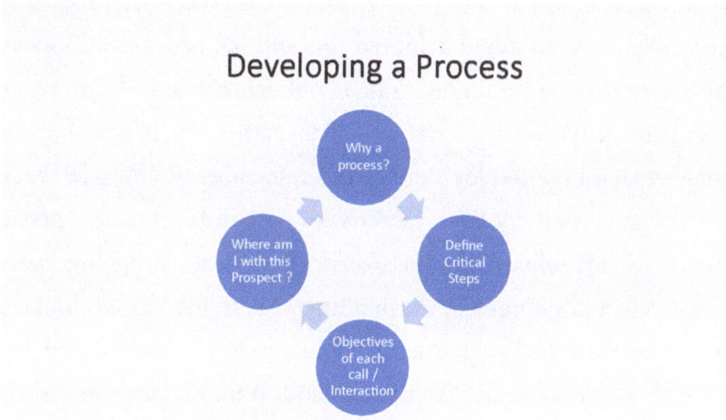

But **It's Not the People It's the Process**

Now to move ahead in Sales Process part i would like to add two important factor which will add flavor in your sales process and that is

1. Attitude
2. Master the art of Tonality

ATTITUDE

After winning the championship award for best employee of the year, I shared my experience and insights with other team members and colleagues on how I achieved this and the principles I follow. So I was giving a presentation in a conference room. As everyone was leaving the room, I was about to gather my things, but for some reason I paused for a moment. I remembered 2006-10 when I had just started my sales career with no hands-on experience in the field of selling products/services. I was struggling very negatively and depressed. At that time, I had just started thinking that I wanted to become a champion in sales and started the journey with my own try & error method. It took a long time (since I had started the journey at my own level) and I had the honor of receiving the Champion award! "How did it happen" I thought to myself and leaned towards being trainable and teachable. The answer came to me loud and clear. I changed my ATTITUDE.

You see, if you change your attitude, sparks fly in the universe. You have energy. You begin to see new possibilities. You set yourself in motion. You achieve extraordinary results. That's why I say when you change your mindset about your revenue growth, you grow exponentially and change your life. It would be a joke if I told you that the last 15 years have just been a string of successes, far from it. I have had my share of defeats and setbacks along the way. But the success principles I have discussed in this book have given me the courage, guidance and strength to keep going.

Act as if it were impossible to fail. – Dorothea Brande

Take control of your sales

I appreciate that you have taken the time to read this book. It seems that you are interested in developing your incredible potential in the sales profession. However, reading this book is only the first step in building your dream career and living the life you want. If you focus on these ideas and take action to create an exciting breakthrough in your sales journey. You may have seen a statistic that says only about 5% of sales professionals manage to develop successful sales traits that help them become millionaires. There is also another statistic presented by Harvard Business Review

Harvard Business Review   Sign In

informed than ever, with access to a wide range of online resources that help them evaluate products before ever meeting with a salesperson. Another factor may be that sales reps spend too much time doing things that don't directly involve selling. The Sales Mastery 2022 survey found that on average salespeople devoted only 32% of their time to selling—and 68% to non-revenue-producing activities.

The percentage of salespeople meeting their annual quotas fell from 63% to 57% from 2012 to 2019, according to global surveys.

Only 57% of salespeople are able to meet their annual sales goals. What is the reason for this ? After 15 years of experience, I am personally convinced that it depends: It is the few people who apply the success principles discussed in this book on a daily basis. It is the rare people who consistently maintain a positive attitude because they know that their thoughts become their reality. It is the rare person who pays attention to the words they use because they know they are programming their mind for unstoppability, mediocrity, or failure. It is the rare person who has the courage to face their rejection, fears, and hesitations because that is where their potential will unfold - by doing what they are afraid of. They are the rare people who see a silver lining in every dark cloud. And it's the rare people who take on something, see it through with a positive attitude, and have perseverance to get the job done. I challenge you to be one of those rare people and challenge you to take on the challenge to better yourself. You have the potential to become more than you ever dreamed of. You carry greatness within you, and your gratitude is the key to unlocking that potential. Changing my attitude has changed my life. And if a better attitude can do wonders in my life, it can do wonders in yours. I want to leave you with these words from Dr. Charles Swindoll, He captured the essence of attitude and how it determines the direction of our lives (not only professional but also personal) The longer I live, the more I realize the impact attitude has on life. Attitude is more important to me than facts. It is more important than the past, than education, money, circumstances, failures, success, and what other people think or say or do. It is more important than appearance, talent or ability. It determines the success or failure of a business, a community, a religion, a society, a home. The remarkable thing is that we have a choice every day as to what attitude we will take that day. We cannot change our past. We cannot change the fact that people will act in a certain way, we cannot change the inevitable. The only thing we can do is play on the one string we have, and that is our attitude. I am a firm believer that the sales corner depends 20% on what happens to me and 80% on how I react to it. And so it is with you. We are responsible for our attitude - pretty strong words, are they not? Do what Charles Swindell suggests and play on the one string you have - your ATTITUDE, Now is the time to take control of your attitude. Now is the time to make miracles happen in your own sales career and life. Go ahead - believe in yourself, have the courage and perseverance to pursue goals. And above all, never forget that a good attitude is the cornerstone of a successful career in sales. It sets the tone with which you interact with prospects, customers, colleagues and management every day. "I am sure you have heard that you should hire for attitude and train for skills, a statement that is true in sales as well as any other field." So a great attitude will also help you seize opportunities. A great attitude means you show up to work on time and do not leave until you have achieved customer satisfaction. A great attitude means you dress professionally to project a professional image. A great attitude means you follow through on your promises to your prospects, no matter what it costs you in hassle or time. To be great at sales, you need to work on developing all aspects.

In Sales, The only 2 things you can control, first is your action or effort and another one is your attitude. -KP Chaturvedi

Let's talk about TONALITY

Tonality is the way you speak, use your voice and influence people.

It's what makes us distinct from others and can be used to build trust, rapport and credibility with clients or customers.

The importance of tonality in sales comes down to one simple concept:

if your tone isn't right for the situation at hand (or if you're not sure), then everything else about what you say will likely fall flat as well! This means that when it comes time for closing a deal with a client or customer – when they're ready to make a decision –you need them saying yes instead of no!

As you can see the benefit of using right tonality in sales conversations are many.

By understanding the customer better and connecting with them on a more personal level, you will be able to build trust with them and move forward in your sales process.

Tonality is the difference in pitch, speed and rhythm that makes a person's voice sound like theirs.

People with different voices have different tones.

It's important to know how your tone sounds to others so you can connect with them and build trust in order to win their business.

Talk in a natural tone of voice to be understood. You want to come across as more human and less sales-oriented, don't you ?

It may not be easy to slow down at first, but it's worth learning how to slow down, take pauses, and craft your tone to be different from other salespeople. On the other hand, if you sound robotic, like you are reading off a script, do you think today's buyers will notice you? Yes, they will, or maybe they will not because they are too busy sleeping through your soporific presentation.

Sales is a competitive environment, and it's important to stand out from your competitors.

Now we have covered what the tonality factor is, how it influences the customer experience, and how it can help achieve your sales goals. Now that you know how important tonality is in sales, we hope you'll think about it when you approach new customers or talk to existing customers in your sales process!

[One of the best parts of this process from the MAP™ method is to ACT , take action now.

-KP Chaturvedi]

always keep in your unconscious mind about your sales process that should not be just time consuming it must be in the direction of some results producing or solution providing and then practice it."

My personal experience:

I've practically experienced the above concept in my Sales career journey of 15+ years.

The ideas in using the sales process on my sales success are not entirely new (I believe in all that I just explained in this book), rather they are a combination of growth mindset + fusion of my own life experience, skills and wisdom gained in all these years.

So I can say for sure that "**Anyone can become a Champion Sales-person**".

If I can do it, then anyone can do it.

Yes, you too, my friend!

Hope you agree!

So if you mix all these three pillars you will generate a result producing SOLUTION FROM YOUR SALES SYSTEM.

SECTION - 2

CASE STUDIES

1st Chapter

Communicate to Win

"Your wealth, your power, and your happiness improve with your ability to communicate."

- Robert Kiyosaki

Communication plays a very critical role in any kind of Sales Business. If it's not done properly then it can create a gap between you and your prospect/ customer or boss, which leads to miscommunication.

Let's understand it from one of the case study-

Mr. Harshit was working in a Paint company as a Customer Service Executive.

The new retailer barged (his way) angrily through the desk and explained his frustration with a credit limit and service charges in recent order. He explained that the agreed upon service charges per year had unexpectedly increased even though it had been locked in the past years.

Harshit quickly realized that the issue had arisen due to poor communication during the deal closure.

Executive Summary

As Discussed in this case study Harshit customer was frustrated due to a lack of communication about the agreed payment terms and conditions for their deal.

In Addition, he could not communicate accordingly that the terms & conditions will change after 5 years, which resulted in unsatisfied customers. Hence, you must speak about the terms and conditions of the deal to avoid an unfavorable situation.

Limiting Beliefs You may have-

- I do not know how to make a good deal.
- I do not like my job.
- I do not know how to communicate appropriately with my customers.

Growth Mindset Affirmations you may like to have –

✔ Now, I understand why we must communicate adequately.

✔ I love my job.

✔ My customers are satisfied with my customer service.

✔ I can explain everything very well to my customers.

Identify Your gap area:

You May Write your Affirmations here :

1.____

2.____

3.____

4.____

5.____

2nd Chapter

New Vs Old Technology

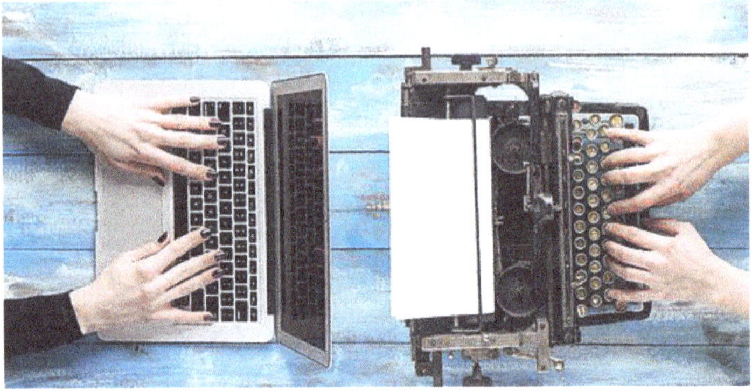

Technology is changing rapidly year on year.

It's very difficult to manage things without upgrading technology.

But the important thing is "don't **waste time on time saving devices.**"

I am nothing against adopting the new technology but you know for the invention of new advancements we led us to science, science led us to technology and technology led us to the wonders of time saving devices, but these days the devices we are using as efficient may be stealing the focus and it led to distractions & losing more time with technology than the time we intended to gain.

Remember this simple truth –

You can either be focused or you can be distracted , but you can never be both at the same time.

According to a report from WEF(World economic forum), on average , in India internet users spend two hours and thirty-six minutes per day on social networking and messaging platforms.

So be careful from this trap, I am not against technology but just keep in mind that we are using technology specially as a front liners for saving time.

One of the best uses of technology for front liners sales professionals is data analysis for identification of your potential customer, network, geography or town.

Data driven sales is one of the essential steps for successful professionals.

Let's discuss a case study: Harshit worked as a Sales Executive in one of the Home improvement

company and one of his customers raised a complaint for Dampness in his bedroom wall. So

Harshit visits the customer place and after taking an overview of the affected wall, he summarizes to his customer that there is a problem in the wall. There is moisture in the wall above the resistance limit of applied paint.

Customer was not accepting the fact and blaming the company for his product performance.

So Harshit was not prepared with his technical kit. So, he told the customer he will come tomorrow with their kit.

And next day he come up with his moisture meter, which can measure the moisture level in the wall

And show to customers that there is a high level of moisture.

Then customers accept the fact and also Harshit realized that the Technology has a tremendous role.

Similarly, many other examples are: you can use technology for collecting and sharing testimonials, network performance.

Executive Summary

As Discussed in the case study of Harshit, to multiply his sales, he used a technique which can save time and increase the sale.

1. You must accept new strategies & tools to enhance your productivity.
2. Ask directions for maximizing your technology tools.
3. Test your technology tool's efficiency.
4. Go backward to go forward : don't use technology if an old, manual method is more efficient.

Limiting Beliefs You may have-

- I am not good at using technology.
- I am not a good sales executive.
- I am not able to attend the customer for his objections.

Growth Mindset Affirmations you may like to have –

✔ I am an efficient Sales Executive.

✔ I am always seeking new technology which can help to increase more sales and enhance customer experience.

✔ My customers trust me.

Identify Your gap area:

You May Write your Affirmations here:

1.____

2.____

3.____

4.____

5.____

3rd Chapter

Take Support

Always remember, you cannot do Everything.

Let's discuss one of my colleagues, Praval He was facing the challenges of providing the accounting details (Transactional Working) to their channel partner.

He was not able to provide all the details on time due to not accessing the CRM in the market and hampering his business. So he took their local office admin support and he defined a system to send all the transactional work to their channel partner before 5th of every month. This activity helps him a lot.

I want to show you one of the biggest surveys done by Proudfoot consulting on work behavior & performance of salesforce effectiveness. Take a look, it was done across the industry

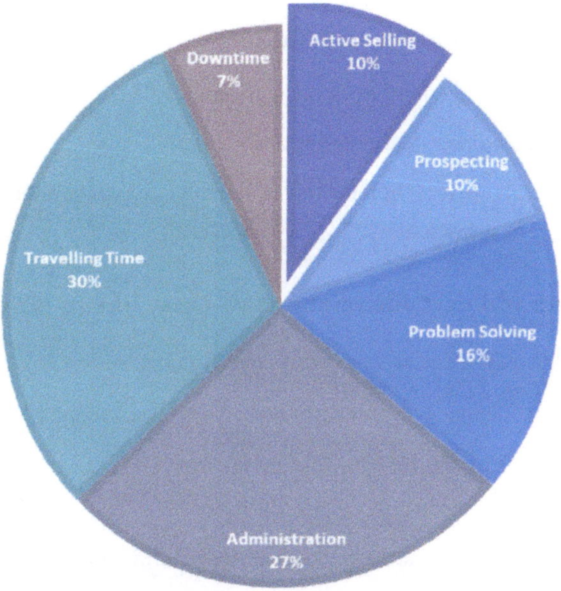

©PROUDFOOT CONSULTING COMPANY

It's clear cut that it's a big trap, where most of the unsuccessful sales professionals are stuck. Clearly it's a problem.

Here's is the secret -

As we discussed in this case study of Praval, he asked for support from his colleagues to improve his territory performance.

Similarly, you must also get help from your coworkers, admin , commercial & IT when needed.

So, if your coworkers have performed exceptionally in your region, you must ask for methods/ productivity secrets they have been using to improve their territory performance .

Limiting beliefs you may have-

- I can not take help from my colleagues.
- My co-workers are not ready to share.
- My territory is not having a potential to grow more than current growth.

Growth Mindset Affirmations you may like to have –

✔ I have an increase in my sales every day.

✔ My colleagues always come forward to assist me.

✔ I am using the method told by my co workers to improve the Sales of my territory.

✔ I am putting every single effort into improving overall time productivity.

Identify Your gap area:

You May Write your Affirmations here:

1.____

2.____

3._______________________________________

4.____

5.____

4th Chapter

Practice of Listening [Listen to Understand]

"Be a good listener," Dale Carnegie advised in his 1936 classic *How to Win Friends and Influence People.*

More than 80 years later, most people still fail to heed Carnegie's sage advice.

- "Frankly, I had never thought of listening as an important subject by itself. But now that I am aware of it, I think that perhaps 80% of my work depends on my listening to someone, or on someone else listening to me."

I can guarantee that in the first and second year of career most of the sales representatives do not care about this factor.

Executive Summary

Are you someone who has a habit of responding all the time?

Be careful if your answer is YES.

you know active listening is far more important in our professional as well personal life journey.

It's playing a big role, people are more distracted in this era. We have social media, all other forms of entertainment like TV, movies, Shows, Video games, and video blogs. There are a lot of ways to be distracted .

Smartphones are another way. Have you ever seen a family eating out at a restaurant and all are looking at a smartphone instance of talking to each other.

Guess what happening in this age of distraction, people are listening less to others.

This is an opportunity for us to improve our active listening skills & this is important for successful sales professionals because if you are going to be friendly with your prospect, connect with people with an emotional level.

if you
listen
better
you'll
sell
more.

3 Levels of it –

1. Listening to Respond.
2. Listening to Understand.
3. Listening to Connect.

Limiting beliefs you may have-

- I do not know how to handle any problem.
- I cannot find an appropriate solution.

- I can not properly connect with my client to close the deal.

Growth Mindset Affirmations you may like to have –

✔ The Solution comes to my mind quickly and effectively

✔ I am happy with making connects with client

✔ I can find an effective and efficient conversation with proper listening.

Identify Your gap area:

You May Write your Affirmations here:

1.____

2.____

3.____

4.____

5.____

5th Chapter

Discovery Phase

If your client/ prospect has any objections in your sales,

A better way to address them is by understanding their needs i.e. pain or desire.

Let's look at the case study, one of my colleagues got success to crack one of the biggest sites in Chhattisgarh through an architect, where they have to supply material for their projects (only one category in Home improvement). But meanwhile he was exploring in depth to understand the total potential(category-wise) of the project.

So going through the process of questioning with focus on escalation of discovery questions , he got to know the exact potential.

Once he got to know, he put all his efforts into value-proposition and was able to convert smoothly with the purchase order of all categories the company was dealing with.

Executive Summary

As you understood the power of the discovery phase with prospect.

Similarly, you must always try to ask more relevant questions to understand the total potential of the project.

You need to talk to your prospect and answer his questions and concerns to get good sales.

Limiting beliefs you may have-

- I don't have questions to ask.
- Why the prospect will answer my question
- What the prospect will think if I ask more questions.
- I don't know how to ask relevant questions.

Growth Mindset Affirmations you may like to have –

- ✔ I am expert at asking open ended questions
- ✔ I can understand what my prospect needs.
- ✔ I can build my clients trust quickly
- ✔ I have the potential to find the solution.
- ✔ I am good at showing good propositions to prospects.

Identify Your gap area:

You May Write your Affirmations here:

1.____

2.____

3.____

4.____

5.____

6th Chapter

Do Not Go With Fix Strategy

You should be careful about making some changes as per conversation with prospects.

So that you can avoid any trouble in the closing deal.

Let's discuss one of the case study

Dheeraj was a newly hired sales executive in our office and was having trouble closing the deal with some of his clients.

Now he decided to ask a coworker for advice on the matter and found that his sales strategy needed to be changed.

The Next time when Vikram was handling the objection of clients, he was more confident and able to answer the queries and close the sale .

Executive Summary

As discussed in the case study of Vikram, he was facing challenges in closing the deal and then he realizes to take advice from his colleague.

After listening to his advice, he was able to understand the actual gap area and got to know the changes needed to make.

Similarly, if you have any area like this in your conversation with prospects, asking for advice and then making changes will be the perfect solution.

Limiting beliefs you may have-

- I can not focus on the gap area.
- I am not good at practically fitting sales strategies.
- I need to change the way I make sales.

Growth Mindset Affirmations you may like to have –

✔ Now I know how to present with clarity to my customers.

✔ Now my customer buys because of the clear picture I present.

✔ I have the best practical Sales Strategy.

✔ I have the potential to close the deal by answering all the queries of clients.

Identify Your gap area:

You May Write your Affirmations here:

1.____

2.____

3.____

4.____

5.____

7th Chapter

Clarification

If you think that your customer does not have clear information about their requirement, It is your primary responsibility to clear their doubts to avoid any loss or low satisfaction level before offering your product /service proposition.

Let's discuss the case study of Bhavik .....

Bhavik found that many of his clients were highly interested to purchase, yet they did not buy for some reason.

To find out why Bhavik needed to see what uncovered objections they had that he hadn't addressed. While talking with a prospect, Bhavik made sure to ask if there was a need for clarification.

When he found an issue that made the client uncomfortable to ask about , Bhavik tried to overcome any potential objections rather than avoid the objections that the client might have had.

In the end Bhavik was able to have a better sales figure because he was able to counter all the objections, even the ones that hadn't been raised.

Executive Summary

As we have discussed in case study, he needed some clarification about any uncovered objections before offering your product/services.

Similarly, if you think you should explain the issues, you must clear them in advance.

Limiting beliefs you may have-

- I am not able to overcome the queries.
- Every customer has always hidden queries.
- I am not getting sales .

Growth Mindset Affirmations you may like to have –

✔ I can clarify all the query.

✔ My sales are getting better every day.

✔ All my customers are ready to purchase.

Identify Your gap area:

You May Write your Affirmations here:

1.______________________________________

2.______________________________________

3.______________________________________

4.______________________________________

5.______________________________________

8th Chapter

Objections

Nothing will ever be attempted

if all possible objections must first be **overcome.**

Let's discuss a case study-

Diwakar was a sales executive at the same company as me. When he was facing challenges in the objections clients had.

Diwakar knew that it was never good to argue with a client, but he was often lost when an objection was raised.

Over time, he learned an excellent method to deal with complaints.

First, Diwakar expects questions and objections. He knew that if the customer were to have difficulties, they would want to see why they should buy.

Second, he welcomed them. He changed the perspective of looking at objections and now he started to take it as a way of probing for information from the customer 's point of view.

Third, He affirmed them. The customer wanted to feel understood, so a simple affirmation went a long way.

Fourth, he made sure to answer questions completely.

Executive Summary

Overcome the objection, and you have a sale.

Limiting beliefs you may have-

- I do not know how to react to the objections of clients.
- I don't have answers for my clients ' questions.
- I don't know the art of dealing with objections.

Growth Mindset Affirmations you may like to have –

✔ Now, I know how to build rapport with prospects.

✔ I have enough knowledge to answer their questions.

✔ I can find a solution for everything.

✔ I can understand the clients point of view.

Identify Your gap area:

You May Write your Affirmations here:

1.______________________________________

2.______________________________________

3.______________________________________

4.______________________________________

5.______________________________________

9th Chapter

Take Commitment "Don't Close".

Everybody has a plan until they get punched in the face.

--Mike Tyson

Unless commitment is made, there are only promises and hopes but no plans.

----Peter Drucker

Create an environment of trust and change the customer conversation at the beginning instead of trying to improve your "closing Skills"

"You must make the customer realize that money they spend is worth it."

As we know that people choose to buy. Nobody ever wants to be sold.

Let's discuss the case study of Viplav ....

Viplav had been trying to close a sale and decided that the deal had to be completed before the client started going outside.

He started to take clients in imagination mode and filled all the benefits then and there with respect to client needs. When the client started asking about things that will happen after sale service and warranty documents.

Biplav knew that it was time to lock the deal. He asked the client the closing question and made sure that the client left feeling confident by reminding the client about the prompt after sale service and paperless warranty (what the client was concerned about).

Both Client and Biplav were happy about the deal.

Executive Summary

As discussed in Biplav case study, he made his client sure that whatever paying is worth it.

Similarly, you must complete the sale without any delay by developing your customers trust so that every time your customer wants to buy anything from you only.

Limiting beliefs you may have-

- I can not make my customer realize that the purchase is beneficial for them.
- My client does not trust me.
- I am not good at rapport building.
- I am not able to close a deal properly.

Growth Mindset Affirmations you may like to have –

- ✔ I know how to close the deal.
- ✔ I am trustworthy for my clients.
- ✔ Now, my customer and I know that this purchase is beneficial for both of us.

Identify Your gap area:

You May Write your Affirmations here:

1. ____
2. ____
3. ____
4. ____
5. ____

10th Chapter

Follow Ups

According to a study by Brevet, 80% of sales require an average of five follow-ups in order to close the deal. However, 44% of sales reps follow up with a prospect only once before giving up. After four follow-ups, 94% of salespeople have given up.

92% of sales pros give up **after the 4th call,**
but 80% of prospects say no four times
before they say yes.

Look at this

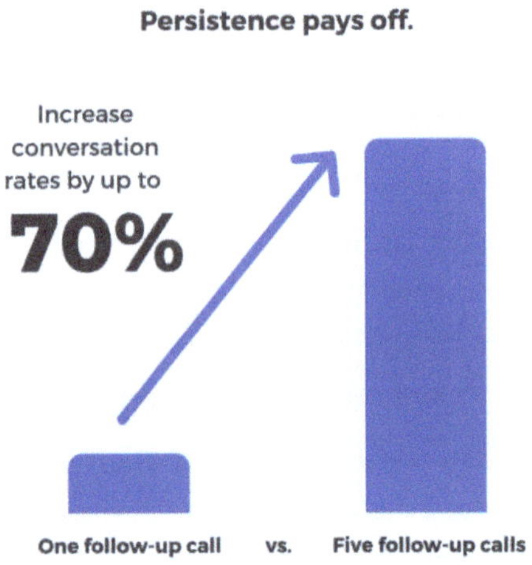

Executive Summary

Plan your calendar accordingly to ensure follow-ups.

Limiting beliefs you may have-

1. It's not my cup of tea to make more and more calls to the same prospect.
2. The prospect will get disturbed if I make a call.
3. The client will call me whenever he will require our product / service.

Growth Mindset Affirmation you like to have-

1. I will close the sale even if I have to take 5+ follow-ups

SECTION - 3

GOALS, COMMITMENT & KPI

Goals……Sales Success & life depends on having worthy goals.

Success is goals and all else is commentary.- By Brian tracy

This is the great discovery throughout all of human history.

Your life only begins to become a great life when you clearly identify what it is that you want, make a plan to achieve it and then work on that plan every single day.

"The primary reason for failure is that people do not develop new plans to replace those plans that didn't work." (Napoleon Hill)

Commit and you will build a legacy

"What this power is I cannot say, I only know that it exists and that it is available only when a man/woman is in that state of mind where he/she knows exactly what he/she wants and is determined not to give up until he/she finds it. - Alexander Graham Bell Having set the goals, I would now like to reveal an important secret, which is the determination to achieve those goals. I always thought I knew that commitment and perseverance meant trying hard. To make many attempts. Commitment is the essence of the ultimate secret. The key to getting what you want is the "Willingness to do whatever it takes" To achieve your goal. Now, before your mind jumps to conclusions, let me add that in swinging "whatever it takes" I am excluding any actions that are illegal, unethical or false commitment to your customers for selling your product/service. So what exactly do I mean by this "willingness"? It is a state of mind that says If it takes 5 steps to achieve my goal, I will take those 5 steps. If it takes 50 steps to reach my goal, I will do those 50 steps. If it takes me 500 steps to reach my goal, then I will do those 500 steps. Of course, at the beginning you will not know exactly how many steps it will take you to reach your goal.

But that does not matter. To be successful, you just need to commit to doing whatever it takes, regardless of the number of steps. How does persistence fit into the picture ? Perseverance follows commitment, which means you have to be committed to something before you persevere to achieve it. Once you are committed to achieving your goals, you will continue with relentless determination and drive until you achieve the desired result. If you make a commitment and are willing to do whatever it takes, Begin to attract the people and circumstances you need to achieve your goal. For example, if you set out to become the best salesperson of the year in your company, you might suddenly come across a potential buyer of your product/service, an influencer, or a triggering event where you have the opportunity to suspect and seek out a qualified customer. It's not like these resources never existed before, it's just that your mind never focused on finding them. Once you set your mind on something, you create a mental picture of what it would be like to achieve it. Then your mind immediately goes to work, like a magnet, attracting events and circumstances that help bring your image into reality. However, it is important to realize that this is not an overnight process, you need to be active and seize the opportunities as they arise.

The magic which flows from commitment has never been eloquently or more accurately described than in the following words by W.H. murray:

As long as one is not committed, there is hesitation, the possibility of setback, always ineffectiveness, in all acts of initiative (and creation) there is an elemental truth whose ignorance kills countless ideas and grand plans: The moment you make a definite commitment, Providence also moves. Here I would like to show you another wonderful characteristic of the power of commitment:

EFFORT ONLY FULLY RELEASES ITS REWARDS AFTER A PERSON REFUSES TO QUIT. –BY NAPOLEON HILL

You do not have to know from the beginning how to achieve your goal. Certainly you are better off if you have a plan of attack, but it is not essential that every step be planned in advance. If you have the willingness to do whatever it takes, the "right" steps will often be revealed to you suddenly. You will meet people you never could have met. Doors will open unexpectedly for you. It may seem as if good fortune or favor is smiling upon you. In truth, you have brought about these positive events by making a commitment and thus directing your mind to seek them. Always remember this quote from Mary Chrowles "One salesperson with a commitment is worth more than 100 people who have only one interest

With ordinary talent and extraordinary perseverance, all things are attainable.

- **Sir Thomas Buxton**

So I am going to get specific with you on goals & not explain their importance or exactly how to set a goal set.

I am going to expect that u already have goals because if u don't know the target you are shooting for then how are u going to hit it.

it's just not possible.

So what I want you to do is take a look at the goal sheet material that's been provided to you as part of this book, take a look at the sheet and start filling in the blanks for annual, monthly as well quarterly goals.

Break down your goals by different categories, so that you understand exactly what you are shooting for.

If you don't know this information write it down, figure it out here or work with your sales manager to understand what your goals should be because sometimes your goals are assigned to you.

However if you really want to win , why not set your goals higher than those that were set for you, don't just decide to go with what someone else thinks you can do.

Why don't you see if you can rise above what someone else thinks you can do?

Top people generally challenge themselves to achieve more & go further than anyone else expects them to do so take this time now to fill out the goal sheet.

I recommend before setting your targets, always look for market potential, it can be 5X, 10X or 100X...........

Goal Sheet-

Complete Your Goal Sheet Now....

1. --

2. --

3. --

4. --

5. --

KPI

KPI's or key performance indicator.

Key Performance Indicators are those items that when you measure them, they help you to reach your GOALS.

I want you to write down your KPIs, look at this sheet, and decide whether or not this list of KPIs is appropriate for you. You should really only agree on 5 to 7 KPIs that matter to you and also to your supervisor or manager so that you are both on the same page when it comes to measuring the right things because if your supervisor wants you to measure this and you over here measure this. That could lead to problems. So you should be clear on a consistent set of KPIs, and in fact it would be best if the entire team was measured against the same KPIs. Of course, you can add your own to the lists that matter to you. So take a look at the sheet with your KPIs and decide which KPIs you want to achieve in a week, a month or a year.

Get your Bonuses (Goals & KPI worksheet) for buying the book by emailing me at

....

SECTION - 4

ACTION, ACTION & ACTION.....

"Well done is better than well said."

-Benjamin franklin

"Action is the real measure of intelligence."

- Napoleon Hill

I like these quotes.

Because really it says it all.

There are two types of salespeople …

One is who love to talk about selling

&

Other sales people are too busy selling to spend much time talking about it.

What type are you??

Giving you a moment to think about that.

Because chances are that if you are not as successful as,

You would like to be you are spending too much time thinking about selling,

talking about selling,

planning to sell Than Actually Selling.

Action replaces thinking about selling & talking about selling.

It's actually picking up the phone ,

it's actually going out

&

looking for prospects.

It's actually sitting down in front of a qualified customers

&

looking for the resale or the upsell .

It is selling so when you think about why you are not succeeding to the level that you like.

You really have to look at your actions,

how r your actions supporting your results …

because if you are taking massive actions

&

you are still not getting the results,

that u would like,

then only you will know .

So the Action is the key.

You know, in India we celebrate the 12 January , the birth of Swami Vivekananda ji as a NATIONAL YOUTH DAY to remember his ideology

You know why ?

Because he always inspired to youth generation for taking action And also one beautiful quote by him is

" Arise, Awake and Stop not until your goal is achieved."

He always says to youths that in this stage of life , if you take actions no one can stop you to achieve your desired goal,

you can do anything ,

you can achieve anything.

He told, if you asked me to choose in these two options

One is playing football and another is reading the Book Geeta. I will go with playing football.

It was all meant to take action.

Because after taking action ,

Action is the only thing which will help you to create an ECCO system for Goals .

E stand for Experience ,

It is one of the best traits in any field . So after taking your first step as action for any idea, plan , strategy , you will be able to get experience.

C stands for Challenges in your path.

Another C stands for Connecting the dots, it will help you to celebrate the small small wins in your journey to staying motivated.

& last is O stand for Objections, only after initiating your sales process means when you start interacting with your prospects & clients then only you will know the real objections.

Do you know the modern world rules for winning?

🎯 It is Fail fast, Fail Cheap

It is not about being the best, it's about being the fastest action taker

So, Be the one who Takes Action Fast

You could be the Best but no one cares if you come Last.

The Most Successful people are not necessarily the best in their fields but they are surely the fastest action takers.

CONCLUSION

That's the 3 Pillars of Millionaire Sellers.

It has helped me and many of my Colleagues and students to clarity their path from

Level of Rejection (Zero) to Level of Champion (Millionaire)

I hope it did the same for you.

In fact,

Before structuring this method, I followed a try & error method for a decade & I was nowhere close to success. It's only in the last 7 years that I cracked the code & learnt the secret.

My results skyrocketed so fast, I became the top salesperson in the company out of hundreds of other reps within 90 days! Mostly what I realized is this: **You can work all the hours under the sun and still end up broke if you don't have the RIGHT skills!** But... When you DO have the RIGHT skills, you'll be able to produce far more than the next salesperson.

Now, all this may sound crazy to you. **But just like Michael Jordan said in his biography, "You can shoot 1,000 jump shots a day, but if your technique is off, *[i.e: if you don't have the right skills]* you're not going to be very good at basketball." The same is true with selling.** Quite simply, Having the RIGHT skills can create automatic success for you - just like it already has for literally thousands of my Colleagues and students!! ***Sales does NOT need to be a numbers game.*** So to sum it all up: All you need to succeed while also working realistic hours, is... **THE RIGHT SKILLS**

To set up your **GAME** plan.

and

Want help developing *RIGHT SKILLS* so you can *enjoy selling*, work less and sell *more* — and make *loads more money*?

If "Yes!", Mail me at kp.chaturvedi@gmail.com & Schedule one on one meeting.

All we really care about is helping you get success.

COMMON ABBREVIATIONS USED IN SALES

CS	CUSTOMER SERVICE
CSR	CUSTOMER SERVICE REPRESENTATIVE
CRM	CUSTOMER RELATIONSHIP MANAGEMENT
BDM	BUSINESS DEVELOPMENT MANAGER
SO	SALES OFFICER
TSO	TERRITORY SALES OFFICER
TSI	TERRITORY SALES INCHARGE
TSE	TERRITORY SALES EXECUTIVE
SS	SALES SUPERVISOR
FIFO	FIRST IN FIRST OUT
SKU	STOCK KEEPING UNIT
DSD	DIRECT STORE DELIVERY
DAVP	DISTRIBUTION AVAILABILITY VISIBILITY PROMOTION
NR	NET REALIZATION (RATE)
POP	POINT OF PURCHASE
B2B	BUSINESS TO BUSINESS
B2C	BUSINESS TO CONSUMER
ROI	RETURN ON INVESTMENT
DPL	DEALER PRICE LIST
SSPL	SUGGESTED SELLING PRICE LIST
MOP	MINIMUM OPERATING PRICE
MTD	MONTH TILL DATE
YTD	YEAR TILL DATE
FAB	FEATURES ADVANTAGE BENEFITS
MS	MARKET SHARE
DSR	DAILY SALES REPORT
RS	REDISTRIBUTION STOCKIST (DISTRIBUTOR)

CD	CASH DISCOUNT
DVR	DAILY VISIT REPORT
VFI	VISIT FREQUENCY INDEX
DD	DIRECT DISTRIBUTOR
SD	SUPER DISTRIBUTOR
QPS	QUANTITY PURCHASE SCHEME
PRI	PRODUCT RANGE INDEX
LPM	LINES PER ITEM
CP	CONSUMER PROMOTION
BOGO	BUY ONE GET ONE
ECO	EFFECTIVE COVERAGE OUTLET
SSMART	SALUTATION SHELF check MERCHANDISING RANGE TAKING order
COC	CODE OF CONDUCT
SOP	STANDARD OPERATING SYSTEM
RC	RETAILER CARD
DHC	DEALER HEALTH (issue status) CARD
AT	ABOVE THE LINE
BTL	BELOW THE LINE
L & B	LEAKAGE & BREAKAGE/DAMAGE
OTC	OVER THE COUNTER
TLSD	TOTAL LINES SOLD PER DAY
LPC	LINES PER CALL
LPI	LINES PER INVOICE
ASV	AVERAGE SITE VALUE
WT	WATER THINNABLE
ST	SOLVENT THINNABLE
RERA	REAL ESTATE REGULATORY AUTHORITY
AID	ARCHITECT /INTERIOR DESIGNER
FR	FIELD READINESS
CFA	CARRYING AND FORWARD AGENT
ROI**	RETURN ON INVESTMENT

ROI ?

Lets understand the Returns on Investment (ROI), the most used calculation for any business.

The key works for this calculation is Returns, earnings, Expenses, Investment.

Here Returns, we call this purely profits. And this is

Returns= Earnings- Expenses

Net Earnings, for example your network partner XYZ Enterprises is doing the business of 10 lacs per month. & suppose the margin in your products is 8% . Then net earnings is

8% of 10 lacs = 80000.

Expense can be direct & indirect.

So Expenses are Staff salary, Rent of Office & godown, Transport charges, Delivery Expenses, Marketing Expenses & other common expenses.

So Assume (you need to calculate as per your requirements) the expenses per month of XYZ is 40000.

So Net Profit= Gross Profits- Expenses

i.e 80000-50000= Rs 30000.

Now Look at the Investment-

The XYZ enterprises invested 10 lacs for average stock maintenance & machinery required.

And their market outstanding is approx. 4 lacs.

So total investment is INR 14 Lacs.

Lets understand it in depth, Since the company is giving 30 days credit & monthly sales is 10 lacs . So it means the actual investment is 4 lacs.

And against the investment of 4 lacs the XYZ is earning INR 30000 per month as return.

So the ROI is

(Returns/ Investment) X 100.

Here ROI= (30000/400000)X 100= 7.5 % per month.

The Annual ROI is = (Total Yearly Earnings/ Investment) X 100

So Annual ROI for XYZ enterprises = (360000/400000) X 100= 90%

REMEMBER TOP 11 PRACTICES OF EFFECTIVE SALES REPRESENTATIVE

1. GET THE KNOWLEDGE YOU NEED
2. **BE A DATA DRIVEN**
3. DEVELOP ACTION PLAN
4. RESPONSIBILITY OF COMMUNICATING
5. ACCOUNTABILITY
6. BE A PROACTIVE RATHER THAN ACTIVE
7. FOCUS ON SETTING CONVERSATIONAL STAGE RATHER MEETING
8. THINK & SAY " WE" rather than " I"
9. Don't CRITICIZE TO COMPETITION (IT ATTRACTS OBJECTIONS)
10. FOCUS ON OPPORTUNITIES RATHER THAN PROBLEMS
11. NO CREDIBILITY- NO SALE

In the end I would like to say that the number one job of a salesperson is solving your customers' problems.

(Remember– "Problem Solvers rule the world".)

ABOUT THE AUTHOR…..

KP Chaturvedi is the founder of Sales Mastery, he has worked for more than 15 years in various industries with top companies. He has helped many sales professionals who have never sold before to become masters in selling. He has made it his mission to empower new sales professionals , Entrepreneurs or who want to learn Sales as a life skill in India and wants to contribute to the Indian government's mission of "Skill India". His core vision is to empower the sales professionals and new entrepreneurs, help them increase their wealth by increasing sales. It is especially helpful for those who are not experts and want to increase their wealth in sales. This book is based entirely on practical experience in front-line B2B and B2C sales.

Notes

Notes

Notes

Notes